ICE BEAR

Nicola Davies

illustrated by **Gary Blythe**

WALKER BOOKS
AND SUBSIDIARIES

LONDON • BOSTON • SYDNEY • AUCKLAND

Polar bears have longer necks and legs than their closest relatives, brown or grizzly bears.

OUR people, the Inuit, call it NANUK.
White bear, ice bear, sea bear, others say.
It's a bear alright, but not like any other!
A POLAR BEAR, made for our frozen world!

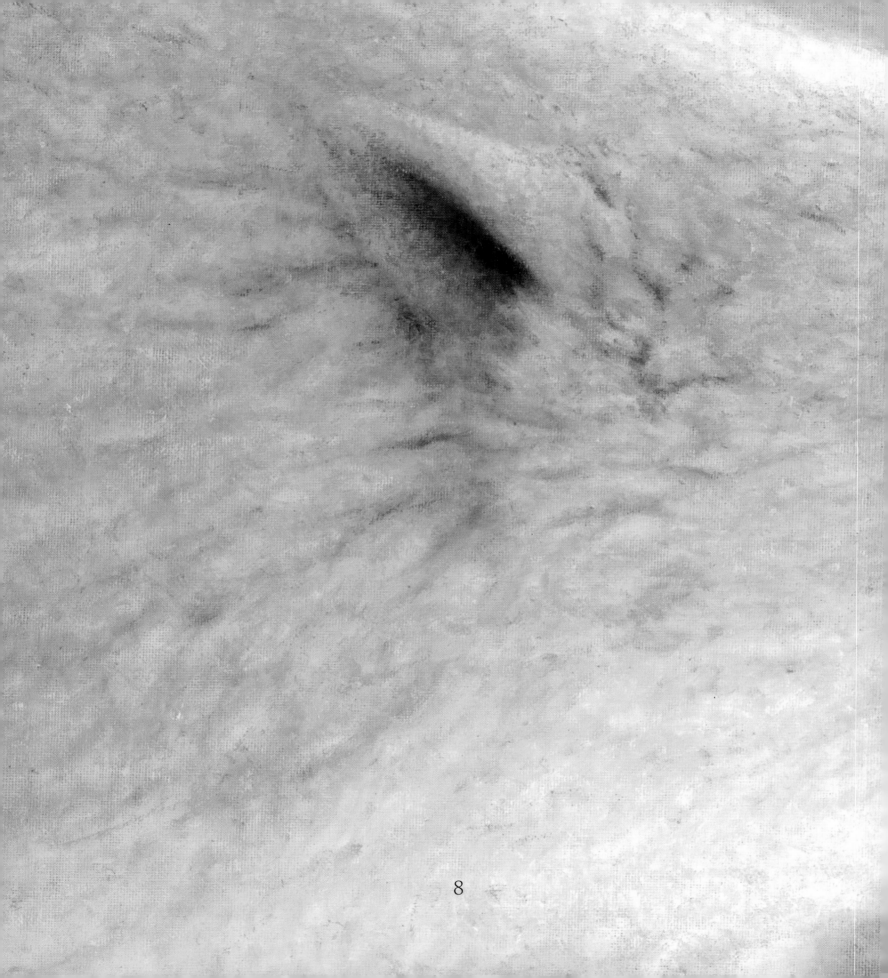

8

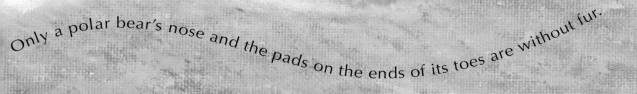

No frost can steal **POLAR BEAR**'s
heat – it has a double coat. One of fat,
four fingers deep, and one of fur
which has an extra trick for
beating cold: its hairs aren't
really white, but hollow,
filled with air, to stop
the warmth escaping,
and underneath,
the skin is black to
soak up heat.

Only a polar bear's nose and the pads on the ends of its toes are without fur.

Polar bears are careful to keep clean so that they stay camouflaged against the snow and ice.

Tiny ice crystals rub the dirt from the polar bear's fur.

Its ears sit close to its head,
neatly out of cutting winds
and its feet are furred for warmth
and grip. So POLAR BEAR
stays warm no matter what.
It will sleep away a blizzard in a drift,
and wash in snow.

Polar bears stay warm in temperatures of minus 40°c and lower.

11

POLAR BEAR is a great hunter.
It outweighs two lions,
makes a tiger look too small...

Polar bears are the biggest hunters on land. Male bears can be three metres long and weigh as much as ten men.

A single paw would fill this page
and shred the paper with its claws.

It can run as fast as a snow buggy
or walk and walk for days on end.
It can swim a hundred miles without a rest
to cross the sea between the ice floes,
then shake the water from its fur and walk again.

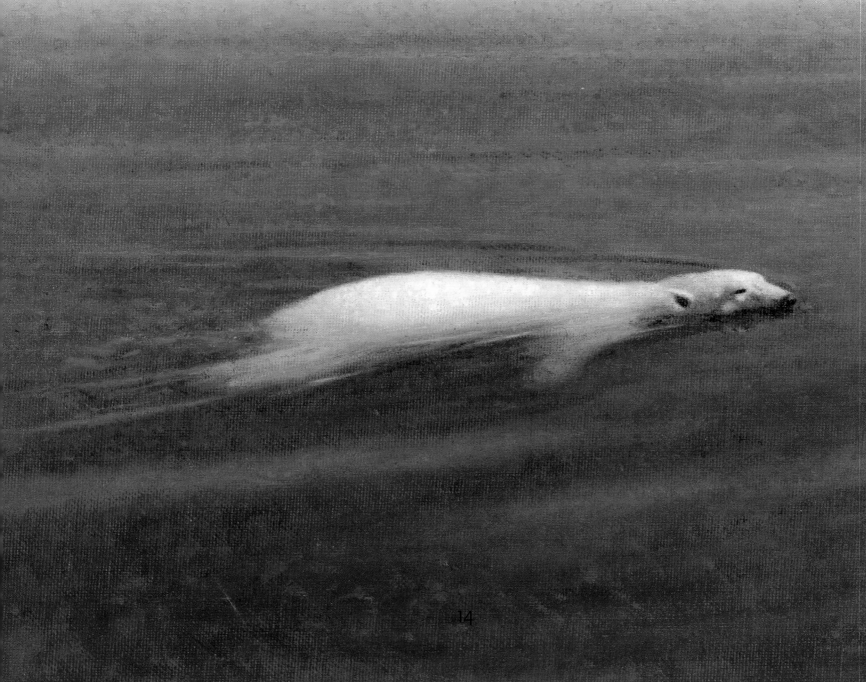

Polar bears' fat keeps them warm in the sea.

Webbed feet help them to swim
and water-shedding fur helps them to dry off quickly afterwards.

Nothing stops POLAR BEAR.

15

Polar bears can only catch seals on the sea ice, so hunting is best in winter and early spring.

Seals are its prey.
It hunts them far out on the frozen sea,
waiting at a breathing hole
or stalking them as they sleep.

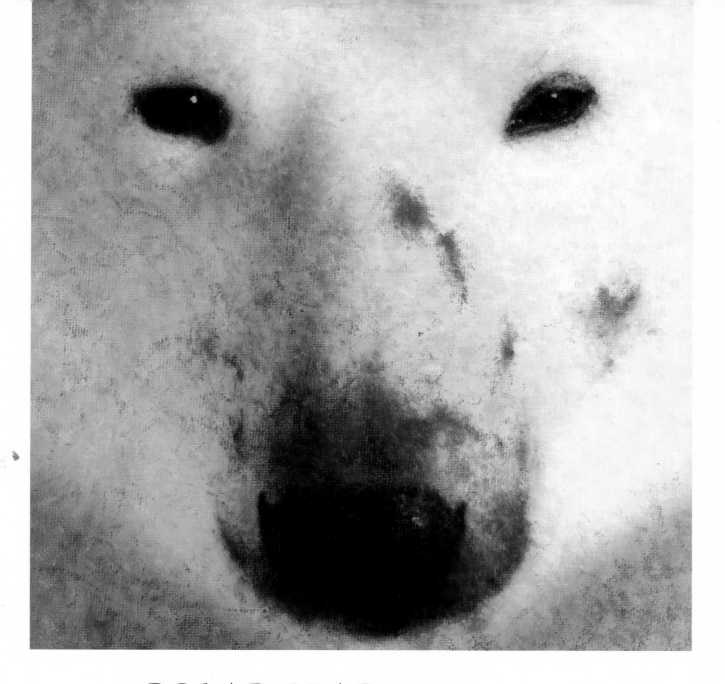

POLAR BEAR is a white shape
in a white world, invisible until it's too late.
A lightning paw strike, a crushing bite
and the seal is gone.

17

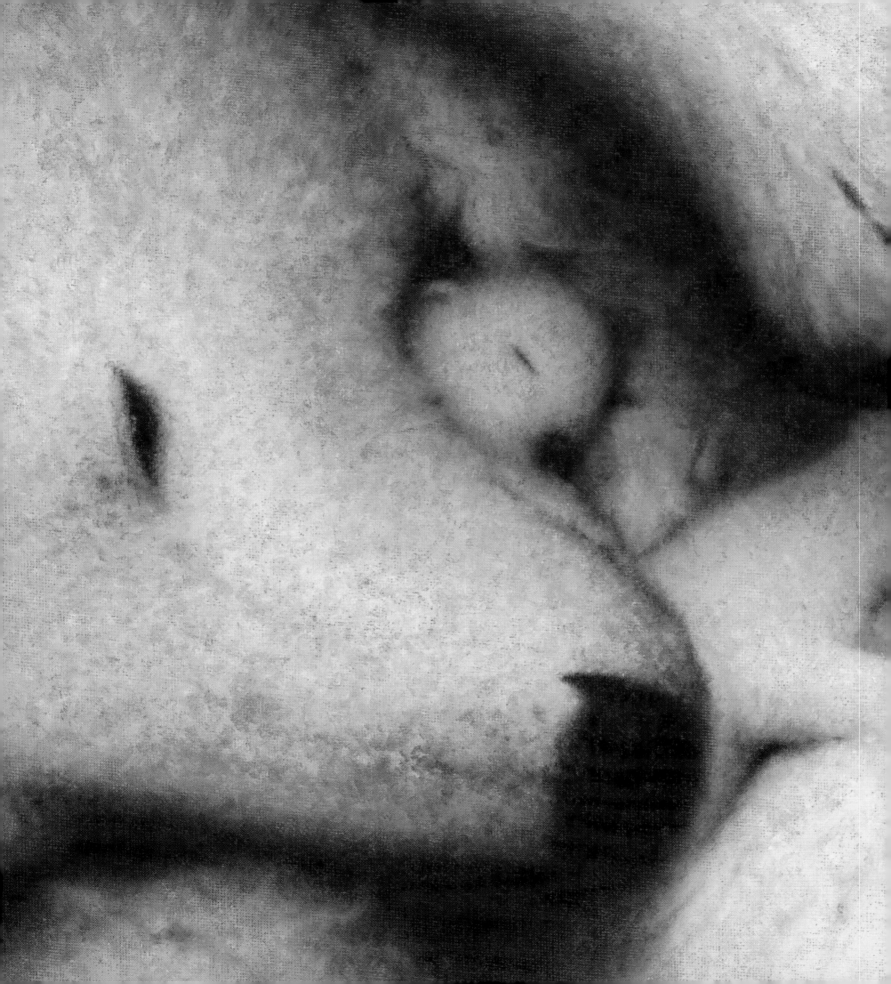

But **POLAR BEAR**
is gentle too.
Mother Polar in her
winter snow den
tends her newborn cubs.
She lifts the tiny bodies
in her great paws
and suckles them.

Newborn polar bears are tiny.
They weigh just 600g – about the same as a guinea-pig!

In spring, she'll take them hunting,
and for two years she'll protect and feed them,
until they've learnt, like her,
to hunt ... alone.

Polar bear mums usually have two cubs at a time,
but sometimes they have one or, very rarely, triplets.

21

ALONE ... through summers when the sun
tracks up and down the sky and one day
passes to another with no night between.

In the Arctic it's light all the time in summer
and dark all the time in winter.

22

When the sea ice melts in summer, polar bears can't catch seals. They'll eat almost anything instead: fish, dead birds, berries, even grass.

ALONE ... through winters when the sun never rises and the stars of the Great Bear sparkle in the darkness.

ALONE ... until the paths
of two lone hunters cross.
They'll wave their heads in
greeting, clasp jaws so tenderly,
they wouldn't break an egg.
Cautiously they'll try each
other's strength.
Then? **Play!**
Giants flowing in the
whiteness, tumbling,
beautiful as snowflakes ...

Real fighting is very dangerous for polar bears!
So males play-fight to find out who's the strongest
without either bear risking getting hurt.

25

Scientists think that when humans came to the Arctic, about 40,000 years ago, they learned how to survive by watching polar bears.

until they part and slowly go their separate ways.

WE Inuit, we watch NANUK,
as we first watched when the Earth seemed new
and POLAR BEAR showed us
how to love the Arctic –
how to hide from blizzards in a house of snow,
how to hunt for seals with patience and with speed,
how to live in starlit day and sunlit night.

Many polar bears and Inuit have passed since then
and still we share our world with gratitude and pride.

27

INDEX

Look up the pages to find out about all these polar bear things.

Don't forget to look at both kinds of word –

this kind and this kind.

ABOUT POLAR BEARS

Polar bears are protected wherever they roam by international agreement. But global warming may be melting the sea ice they depend on. Here are some things you can do to keep polar bears roaming the Arctic:

• Switch off lights, TVs and computers when you don't need them.

• Cycle or walk instead of getting in the car.

Every little bit helps!

ABOUT THE AUTHOR

Nicola Davies is an author and
zoologist. The Arctic is the most
extraordinary place she has ever
been to and she wanted to
celebrate its magic by writing
about the two ultimate Arctic
survivors: polar bears and the
Inuit people. Nicola is also the
author of BIG BLUE WHALE,
ONE TINY TURTLE and POO.

ABOUT THE ILLUSTRATOR

Gary Blythe has illustrated several
picture books for children, but
this is the first non-fiction one.
The majesty of the polar bears
provided him with lots of
inspiration, as well as the chance
to work with a whole new range of
brighter colours. Gary has recently
illustrated Bram Stoker's DRACULA,
adapted by Jan Needle.